CW01604712

TALES OF THE BORDER REIVERS

SANDHILL
PRESS

First published in Great Britain in 1995.
Reprinted 2000

This book incorporates some material first published in 'Rogues and Reivers of the North Country' *published in 1990 and the copyright of Sandhill Press.*

17 Castle Street, Warkworth,
Morpeth
Northumberland, NE65 OUW.

ISBN 0 946098 50 6

Tales of the Border Reivers selected and retold by staff at Sandhill Press.

Designed by Sandhill Press, set in Palatino 11pt.

Cover photograph courtesy of Hartnell Images.

Printed by Martin's the Printers,
Berwick upon Tweed.

CONTENTS

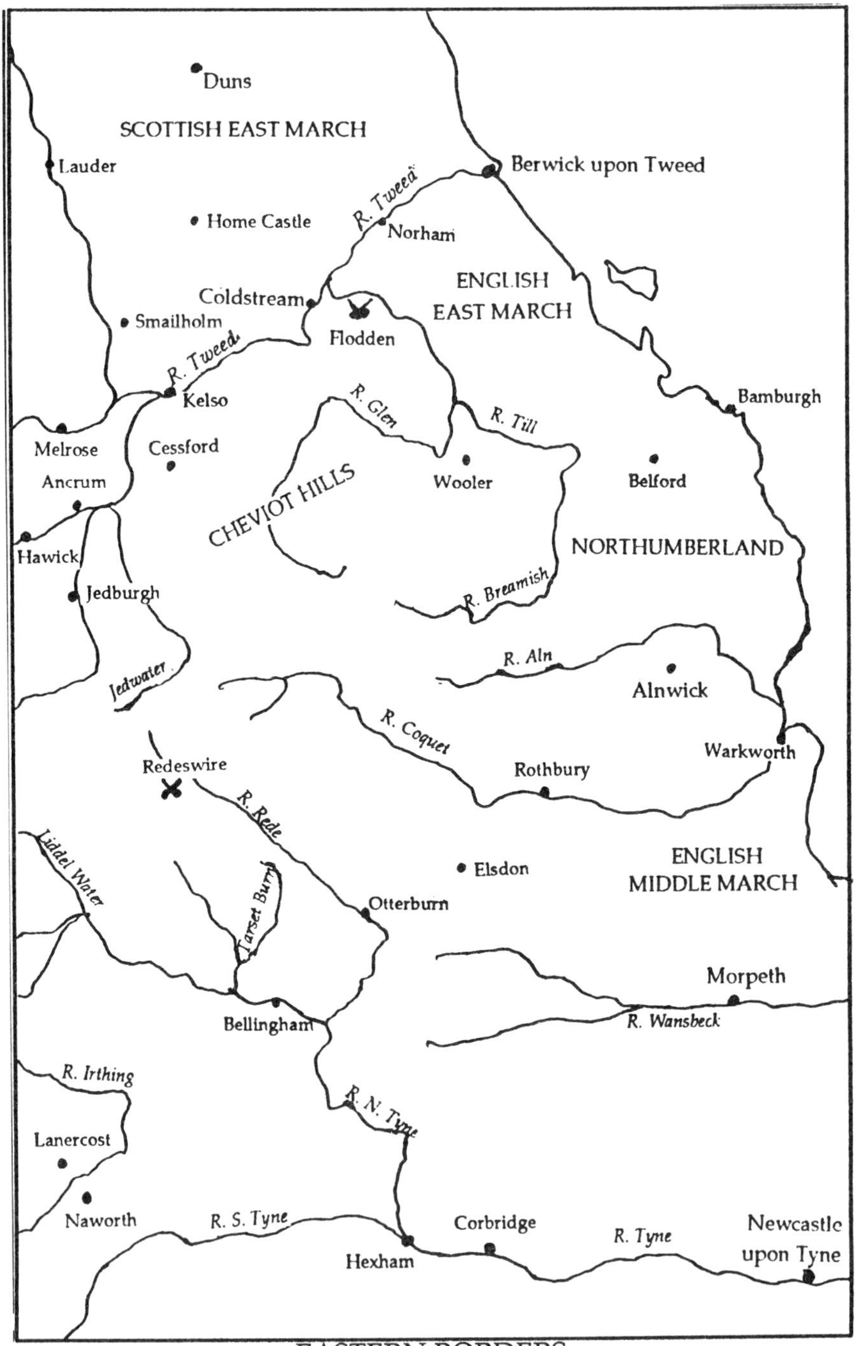

EASTERN BORDERS

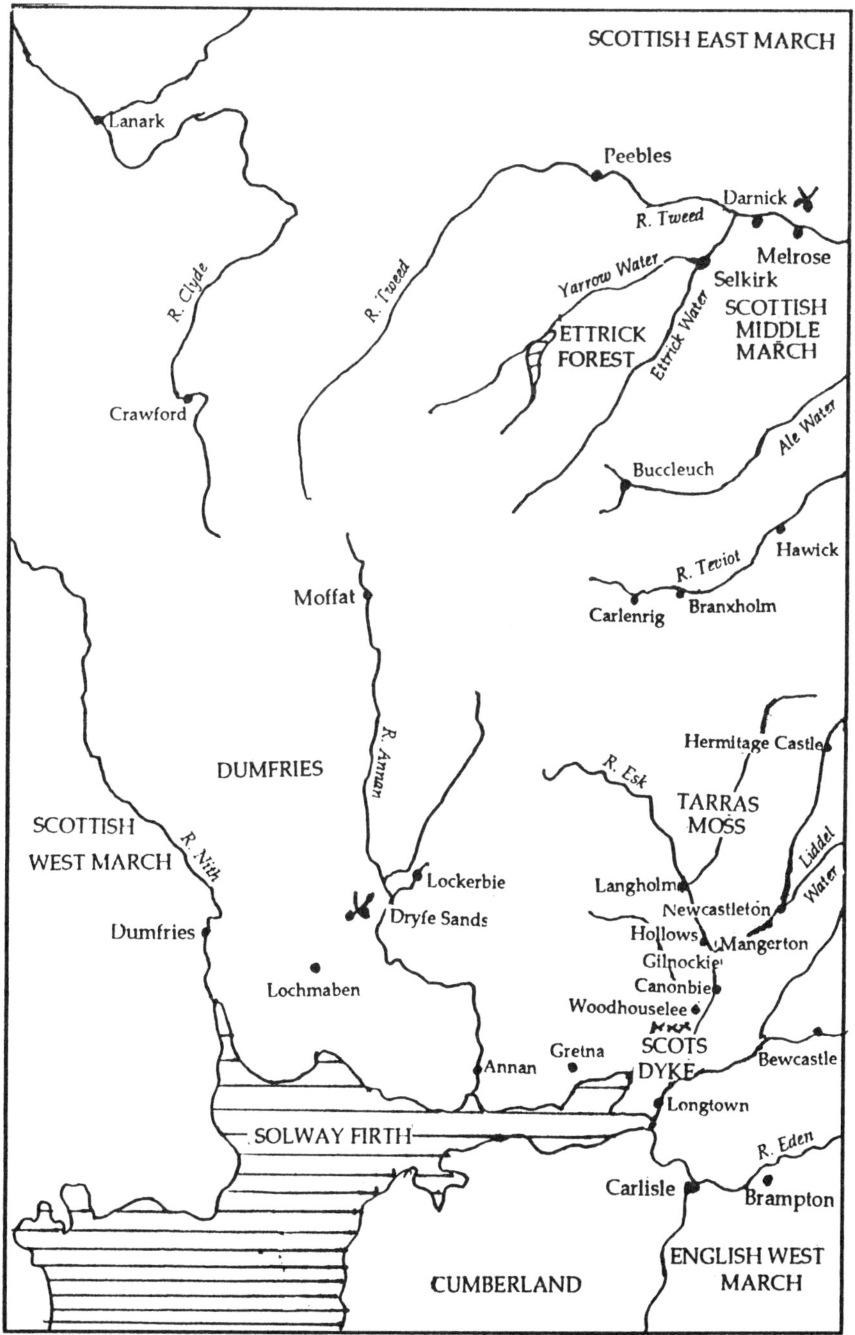

WESTERN BORDERS

SOME REIVERS FAMILY SURNAMES

ARCHBOLD
ARMSTRONG
BEATTIE
BELL
BURNS
CARLETON
CARLISLE
CARNABY
CARRS
CARRUTHERS
CHAMBERLAIN
CHARLTON
CHARLETON
COLLINGWOOD
CRISP
CROSER
CROZIER
CUTHBERT
DACRE
DAVISON
DIXON
DODD
DOUGLAS
DUNNE
ELLIOT
FENWICK
FORSTER
GRAHAM
GRAY
HALL
HEDLEY
HENDERSON
HERON
HETHERINGTON
HUME
IRVINE
IRVING
JOHNSTONE
KERR
LAIDLAW
LITTLE
LOWTHER
MAXWELL
MILBURN
MUSGROVE
NIXON
NOBLE
OGLE
OLIVER
POTTS
PRINGLE
RADCLIFFE
READE
RIDLEY
ROBSON
ROUTLEDGE
RUTHERFORD
SALKELD
SCOTT
SELBY
SHAFTOE
STOREY
SIMPSON
TAILOR
TAIT
TAYLOR
TROTTER
TURNBULL
WAKE
WATSON
WILSON
WOODRINGTON
YARROW
YOUNG

THE RAIDERS

Last night a wind from Lammermoor came roaring up the glen
With the tramp of trooping horses and the laugh of reckless men
And struck a mailed hand on the gate and cried in rebel glee:
"Come forth! Come forth, my borderer, and ride the March with me!"

I said "Oh! Wind of Lammermoor, the night's too dark to ride,
And all the men that fill the glen are ghosts of men that died!
The floods are down in Bowmont Burn, the moss in fetlock deep;
Go back, wild Wind of Lammermoor, to Lauderdale - and sleep."

Out spoke the Wind of Lammermoor, "We know the road right well,
The road that runs by Kale and Jed across the Carter Fell.
There is no man of all the men in this grey troop of mine
But blind might ride the Borderside from Teviothead to Tyne!"

The horses fretted on their bits and pawed the flints to fire,
The riders swung them to the South full faced to their desire;
"Come!" said the Wind from Lammermoor, and spoke full scornfully,
"Have ye no pride to mount and ride your father's road with me?"

A roan horse to the gate they led, foam-flecked and travelled far,
A snorting roan that tossed his head and flashed his forehead star;
There came the sound of clashing steel and hoof-tramp up the glen
...And two by two we cantered through, a troop of ghostly men!

I know not if the farms we fired are burned to ashes yet!
I know not if the stirks grew tired before the stars were set!
I only know that late last night when Northern winds blew free,
A troop of men rode up the glen and brought a horse for me!

Will H. Ogilvie

This poem was first published in *'The Border Poems of Will. H. Ogilvie'* by John Murray Head in 1959. While this was not written in the Border Ballad tradition, Ogilvie, himself a Borderer, brings to life the stirring times which are related in this book.

A BORDER WAY OF LIFE

"Mountainous and strange is the country,
And the people rough and savage."

It is not surprising that people living near a frontier find themselves subject to the territorial ambitions of those in power, the English and Scottish Border being no exception. Borderers from both countries had sprung from the same mixture of races, spoke a similar language and shared many characteristics. Although disorder and unrest had prevailed from earliest times, it was Edward I's determination to bring Scotland to heel that was the turning point in the battle for control of the Border country.

This explosive situation was encouraged by Henry VIII and by the middle of the sixteenth century the bid for survival in the Border area took on a new meaning. People who had fought and struggled through the war years had learned to live rough, moving on at a moment's notice and obtaining food by fair means or foul.

After the Battle of Flodden in 1513 and the defeat of the Scots, Henry tried to bring peace to the Borders, but men who had been encouraged to rob, kill and steal were not now inclined to settle for the hard life trying to make a living from farming. Instead they took to robbing other people of cattle and goods - the heyday of the 'Border Reivers' had begun.

The ancestors of the thousands of people who today bear the names of Armstrong, Charlton, Graham, Scott, Elliot and others, were united within their clans or surnames and could often call upon hundreds of men of the same 'grayne' to join them for forays across the Border in search of cattle and goods. The reivers, as law breakers, were virtually unique in that they came from all classes, not just a minority group, and all lived by the same violent code. The families or surnames, produced fearless men who admired courage and strength and knew no other way of life but breeding livestock which, if lost, they simply replenished from another's herd.

Rough temporary shelters, known as shielings, could be built in 3 or 4 hours and involved planting a few stakes in the ground, filling the gaps with stones and turf. The walls were furnished with brushwood and mud with branches laid across to make a roof. Wooden shutters were provided for the unglazed windows and the door was usually made of cow hide. These dwellings, while providing rudimentary shelter, offered little protection against the enemy.

It was the stone built peels, (more prominent in the 16th century as stone replaced clay), usually the homes of chieftains and their families, which provided a more adequate defence. These were three or four storeys high with thick stone walls, which offered protection against the enemy, especially from the risk of fire. A large surrounding wall known as a barmekin provided shelter for people and cattle. Should the family have to abandon the peel under the threat of an invasion, the interior of the tower was packed with smouldering peat which burned for days and made it impossible for gunpowder charges to be laid, or for attackers to gain entry. On his return, although he had to make some repairs, the Borderer's tower had suffered little damage.

The ground floor of the peel provided stabling for the animals, with the living room and bedrooms on the higher levels. There would normally be a clan bell or beacon in the roof to raise the alarm. As a result of the constant threat of fire and plunder, interior furnishings were kept to a minimum with very few luxuries.

The 'bastle' or 'bastle house' was a cheaper alternative to the peel but was longer and narrower, the walls being about half the thickness, and there was no barmekin.

Clothing also consisted of the bare essentials for the simple Borderer, but the more wealthy may have owned luxurious velvet and satin gowns, breeches and jackets. The typical reiver, while on his illegal raids, wore a steel bonnet, or bowl-shaped helmet, and a jack or jacket, which was well padded and sewn with metal plates, but was lighter than armour. They often carried bows and arrows and, as progress was made, a dag or heavy hand gun. Their favourite weapon, of which the reiver was an expert, was a lance used for thrusting and throwing. Also vital to their survival was the Border horse, a small active animal capable of negotiating the difficult terrain, made treacherous with many bogs and marshes.

Food eaten at home consisted of meat, cheese and barley, with vegetables being in short supply, and little bread available. The women usually tended small vegetable plots which yielded barely enough to feed a family, therefore reiving was, in fact, a means of survival. The Borderer did not consume much wine or beer, and drunkeness is seldom mentioned in Reiver history. While out on their unlawful sorties, the raiders ate animal flesh and carried oatmeal which was mixed with water and heated on a metal plate to make a thin cake.

One famous tradition of the reiver way of life is often related. When food stocks were running low or the larder was bare, the lady of the household sent the menfolk to replenish it. The wife of one of the Graham clan, for example, used to greet the hedesman (or chief) with the following words: *"Ride, Rowley ride. Hough's i' the pot."* The hedesman of the Charltons of Hesleyside would be confronted at breakfast by a large dish which, when uncovered, revealed a single spur. The spur has been in the possession of the Charltons for centuries as their family dates back to the early Middle Ages.

The following description is given in Richardson's 'Local Historian's Table Book':

"The spur is about six inches in length; the breadth of the heel from stud to stud three inches and nearer the back of the heel two and a quarter inches. The length from either stud to the back of the heel three and a quarter inches; from the shoulder to the knee one and a quarter inches; and from the knee to the rivet of the rowel, one and three quarter inches. The rowel is two inches in diameter." (The Charlton Spur still exists at Hesleyside - see Godfrey Watson's book 'The Border Reivers.')

As far as recreation was concerned, the reivers enjoyed poetry and music, singing ballads to the accompaniment of the harp or pipe, or playing the small pipes. The poetry consisted of long melancholy epics, passed down by word of mouth, concerned with the realities of life and death - there were few happy endings.

Gambling, not surprisingly, was in the reivers blood and hunting and hawking provided exercise when they were not fighting each other. Football was enjoyed by all and the Armstrongs particularly enjoyed the game, a star player being Wat Armstrong. Even a friendly football match, however, could end in violence. In 1599 six Scottish Armstrongs visited Bewcastle to play a match against six Englishmen. On hearing news of this event William Ridley saw the opportunity to capture the Armstrongs. The plotters, however, were overheard by Francis Forster of Kershope Foot, who forewarned the team and arranged an ambush during which they cut the throats of Ridley and of Nichol Welton, killed one of the Robsons and captured thirty prisoners.

The reivers greatest recreational indulgence, however, was horse racing. At a time when a man's life depended on the speed and staying power of his horse, the beast assumed a great importance and owners were proud of the animals and their own skill. Race meetings proved to be most popular in the West Marches and those particularly addicted to the chase included Kinmont Willie and his kinsman, the Lord of Mangerton.

It may seem all too easy to see the Border Reivers in a romantic light. Events took place so long ago and have been embroidered and recorded in ballads, and 'heroes' have sprung up such as Kinmont Willie, Jock 'o' the Side, Johnny Armstrong etc. In reality, the Border way of life in the sixteenth century was hard and cruel, a daily battle against fear of raids and plunder, a basic struggle for survival in a lawless environment.

England and Scotland had always had separate legal systems, but along the frontier it was necessary to have some form of international law. The origin of Border Law, or *Legis Marchiarum*, can be traced to a conference of November 1248 when six English and six Scottish knights met *"and corrected, according to the ancient and approved custom of the March, such matters as required to be redressed."*

A written code of thirteen articles was agreed the following year when twelve knights sat on each side. The main points to be laid down were that fugitives should be returned to their respective countries for the recovery of debts, and that accused persons should be summoned to answer for their crimes at a fixed place on the Border. This was the origin of the 'Day of Truce' (see page 19).

As well as conforming to the ordinary laws of his country and the by-laws of his particular barony, the Borderer must also abide by the Border Laws, the breaking of which constituted 'March Treason', punishable by death.

The main offences to which the law applied were murder, theft, assault, robbery and arson. The nature of the frontier meant that normally minor incidents such as cattle grazing, hunting and fishing, and ploughing and sowing also gained a high legal profile.

The Border Laws were amended, added to and reviewed over the next three centuries by English and Scottish peace commissioners and by local agreement.

Actually enforcing the laws was more difficult as co-operation between the officials was by no means perfect, and there was a distinct lack of law enforcement. There was little improvement by 1596 when the last Border Law was published.

The following is a summary of the more important laws:-

MURDER

If an Englishman violently killed a Scot, the English warden should try to arrest the offender and bring him to the Day of Truce. (By the middle of the sixteenth century the penalty for murder was almost certainly death.) If convicted, the man would then be delivered to the Scots warden for execution. All the 'moveable' goods of the murderer were delivered to the bereaved family for their 'use and profit'. The same, of course, applied when a Scot murdered an Englishman.

ASSAULT

Subjects of either realm who were unlawfully wounded by someone from the opposite realm could make a 'bill of complaint' at the Day of Truce. If the bill was filed, twelve gentlemen 'of worship and good fame', six from England and six from Scotland, selected by the respective wardens, estimated the damage.

RAISING FIRE

Those who burned or 'spoyled' goods in the opposite realm had to make payment of 'double or sawfie'. 'Double' simply meant paying twice the value of the damage and 'sawfie' was an extra payment to reimburse the authorities for the expense of the collection.

HUNTING

No subject of either realm could enter the other country for hunting, fishing, hawking etc. without the owner's consent. Hunting provided recreation and in the more quiet times the Scots asked permission to hunt in the Forest of Cheviot. However, during the last years of Sir John Forster's wardenship, the Scots, taking advantage of his advancing years, hunted without permission. They also cut wood which was strictly forbidden according to Border Law.

PASTURING CATTLE

Up until 1522 it was common for Borderers to graze their cattle on the other side of the Border, provided that they brought them back before sunset. After this date, however, any stock found on the wrong side of the Border were impounded and the owner had to pay 'parcage' to release his animals.

'BAUCHLING'

Bauchling was a public reproof, usually taking place at a Day of Truce, and involved the display of a glove (representing the false hand of the person bauchled) on the end of a spear. The offender was accused or challenged for breaking his word or bond. Originally, the offender's name was shouted at the assembly which usually made him pay up or fight. If he did not, he may have been executed by those of his own clan to remove the disgrace. As a result of this, the Treaty of 1553 forbade the practice of bauchling except by licence of the wardens.

PERJURY

Perjury was once a capital offence but was later punished by imprisonment. If anyone swore to a man's innocence, yet knew him to be guilty, he was taken to the opposite warden to be imprisoned for a year and a day, and must then appear at the next Day of Truce. Perjurors were publicly declared liars before the wardens and declared to be men in whom no trust should be placed.

COLD TROD

(see also 'The Hot Trod' page 26)

This related to the recovery of stolen goods and meant that the injured party did not require safe conduct into the opposite realm so long as the trail was followed within six days and *"the first honest man inhabiting within the Marches which he hath entered"*, witnessed the pursuit.

FUGITIVES

Fugitives and rebels who crossed from one country to the other, together with anyone who harboured them, were dealt increasingly severe penalties. Indeed, those who were found sheltering fugitives were often given the death penalty.

CAPTURE OF FORTALICES

If anyone from either realm should capture a fortress in time of peace, the owner may recover it, by force if necessary, as soon as possible. The wardens of the country whose subject took the fortress were bound to aid the owner or the owner could 'require' them to return the fortress to him.

LAW AND ORDER: THE WARDENS OF THE MARCHES

"I oft have heard of Lydford Law,
Where in the morn men hang and draw,
And sit in judgement after."

❖❖❖❖❖

The lands on both sides of the Border were divided into the East, West and Middle Marches and, by the early fourteenth century, these were under the authority of Wardens. In Scotland, the East March consisted of the eastern part of Berwickshire and was mainly dominated by the Home family. The English equivalent included all the north east part of Northumberland. The western boundary ran from the Cheviots to the River Aln and was under the general influence of the Earls of Northumberland.

The Middle March, administered from Alnwick, consisted of the rest of Northumberland and included Tynedale and Redesdale. The Scottish Middle March contained the rest of Berwickshire and the whole of Roxburghshire, extending as far north as Peebles. Kirkcudbright, Annandale and Dumfries made up the Scottish West March, and the English side covered Cumberland and Westmoreland, with headquarters at Carlisle Castle.

Although the wardens were first heard of in 1318, they may well have existed earlier. The government of the Marches was in their hands and at first there was only one Warden General on each side of the Border with most of the work done by deputies. Later, this system expanded and three wardens ruled on each side together with keepers, land sergeants and bailiffs. Concerned at first only with defence, the wardens gradually became responsible for capturing criminals, administering the Hot Trod (see page 26), collecting fines, holding warden courts and sessions etc.

The wardens had wide powers and were expected to administer the area with little help from central government. Although in theory, offences against the ordinary laws of the land were dealt with in the justice courts, while the wardens dealt with the Border Laws (see page 9), in practice the wardens had total authority within the area, with powers of life and death over people. Co-operation with the opposite warden was an important part of their duties.

Salaries varied but an English warden could be paid between £300 and £1100 sterling annually, where as a Scottish warden may receive £100 a year which was equivalent to £20 sterling. (The Scots pound was worth about four English shillings).

In Scotland there was a tendency for wardens to come from the same families: in the East March the warden was usually a Hume, in the Middle March a Kerr and in the West March, the Maxwells had control. There was more reluctance on the English side to appoint local nobles and by the end of the sixteenth century it was most likely that a non-Borderer would be appointed. Sir John Forster was the only true exception as a local warden on the English side.

There were advantages and disadvantages to these appointments. On the one hand, a local man knew the area and the people, but on the other, he might become too involved in local feuds and have little regard for central government. An outsider had the obvious problem of not knowing the area or the people, and he may have had somewhat erratic support from central government.

Inevitably co-operation between the opposite wardens was not all it should have been as they rarely trusted each other and were often personal enemies. They were manipulated by their respective governments to harass and spy on the other side. As long as national interests were served, the local needs of the Borderers were of little concern.

Whatever he did, the warden was in a difficult position. If he was too tough he could antagonise local chiefs and landowners, but on the other hand, should he not show authority, his March could become uncontrollable. Scottish wardens, because of lack of support from central government and no back up from state troops etc., had less control over the natives than their English counterparts.

Although many offenders were arrested, a network of spies and informers often ensured the reivers escape. Suitable prisons and towers were in short supply and often in a poor state of repair, such as at Hexham and Harbottle. This, together with the divided loyalties of the gaolers who often belonged to a particular surname, meant that there were many escapes, particularly in England.

In 1518 Lord Dacre arrested ten thieves from Redesdale and escorted them to Rothbury en route for Morpeth gaol, hoping there would be someone brave enough to testify against them. Spies informed the men of Redesdale of the arrest and they crossed the moors to Simonside, overtaking the party in Rothbury Forest. They ambushed the eighty strong escort, killing the bailiff and six others, and taking the gaoler and four men prisoner, before disappearing over the moors to take refuge in Scotland.

On another occasion prisoners from Tynedale reached Morpeth where their fellow reivers attacked the gaol and rescued, among others, Cokes Charlton - *"the most notable thief in that country."*

Due to the number of escapes from Hexham gaol, special precautions were taken to protect prisoners from rescue by the men of Tynedale. One night a number of guards described as *"simple, poor men without harness or good weapons"*, left their posts, leaving only a few men on duty. At midnight a large force of reivers entered the prison, attacked the remaining guards and freed the prisoners. They included Clem Armstrong, and the notorious villain, Jerry Charlton, nicknamed 'Topping' for his distinctive tuft of hair. He later endured a spell of imprisonment in Warkworth Castle, and was the only survivor of a particularly rife outbreak of the Plague.

Escape from Carlisle Castle seemed to be equally easy. In 1605, for example, 29 out of 33 condemned prisoners broke out, including a number of Grahams and Armstrongs. On one occasion, Sir Thomas Wharton, warden of the West Marches, agreed with James V to exchange Andrew Bell for prisoners held in Scotland. Preparations were made for the ceremony but Bell was found to have escaped and was eventually discovered on the other side of the Border. Bell had apparently been given liberty within the castle, and professing to an interest in religion, persuaded the captain of the castle to take him to church. When the captain was given the order for the exchange, Bell feigned illness and was put in the lodge to recover. Two days later a gaoler left the door open after delivering supper and Bell, seizing his chance to escape, jumped the lodge wall and was gone.

Intelligence gathering and espionage played an important part in the wardens' work and extensive spy networks were operated. The Scots were particularly efficient in this field and there was little that took place in England that they did not know about.

One of the greatest English spy masters was Sir Francis Walsingham who gathered intelligence from a wide area. He achieved an important breakthrough from a relatively minor Border incident. In 1582 three of Sir John Forster's men discovered a man who refused to give his name and he was arrested. They took his luggage, which included a set of dentist's instruments and a looking glass, and, after he had offered them a bribe, they released him.

Forster heard of this and imprisoned the three men, taking the goods removed from the fugitive. Having given the items a casual look he noticed some paper in the looking glass and subsequently discovered certain letters written in code, and hidden within the glass.

He despatched the glass and letters to Walsingham to be examined by his code breakers who discovered a reference to the 'Enterprise of England', King Philip II of Spain's name for the Spanish Armada. The rest, as they say, is history...

DAYS OF TRUCE

"Our wardens they affixed the day,
And as they promised so they met."

❖❖❖❖❖

The task of the wardens to enforce law and order amongst the Border reivers within their respective Marches was both difficult and dangerous. Crimes committed within a particular March could be tried in the warden's own court when the offender was arrested within his area of jurisdiction. It was more difficult, however, attempting to arrest a man in another country i.e. in a March across the Border.

The solution was to hold regular meetings between a warden and his opposite number where they could exchange the prisoners that each wanted.

The first meetings were held in 1248 and 1249 when complaints arising from raids, thefts, murders and kidnapping were heard.

These Days of Truce should have been held once a month but they actually occurred at the convenience of the particular wardens, who would often postpone a meeting for tactical purposes, or simply not turn up.

The meetings were held at a town rather than on the March, at Jedburgh, Kelso, Alnwick or Carlisle for example. From sunrise of the meeting day to sunrise of the next day an armistice was declared and every man attending was supposed to have safe conduct.

The Days of Truce were regarded rather like a Bank Holiday and spectators would arrive from far and near, armed, but with no intention of using their weapons. Everyone would be in their best clothes as pedlars and tinkers set out their stalls: old scores temporarily forgotten.

It must have been quite a sight as the English and Scottish wardens, at the head of their entourages, came into view and surveyed each other across a burn or valley. Familiar faces would be spotted : old enemies with whom they may have recently fought.

According to custom, the English warden would then send one or two of his riders across to the Scottish side and ask for the assurance that peace be kept until the following sunrise. This was essential as it ensured that everyone would arrive home safely before the truce expired.

The Scottish warden, having given his assurance, then sent his own men to seek the same of the English warden. Having received this, the two men would hold up their hands in a token of good faith. Only after this, would the English warden and his party enter the Scottish ground where the two wardens traditionally embraced each other.

Some wardens adhered strictly to the rules whereas others, such as John Forster, were more relaxed. He held meetings either side of the border according to convenience. In 1586 when there was a considerable amount of business to deal with, he drew lots with the Scottish warden and the six days of truce were divided between Alnwick and Kelso.

Normally, however, the business took place on the Scottish side of the border and it was customary for the English to enter Scotland. One reason for this was that after a war the Scots first demanded peace, and in peace time it was the English who first demanded the assurance.

Once business began a jury of twelve were chosen, six Scots chosen by the English warden and vice versa. Only 'respectable' men should have been sworn in, but owing to the nature of family relationships and the company gathered there, this must have been a little difficult!

Bills of complaint were looked at and the accused summoned to answer them. A trial may then have been necessary and these took various forms. One was that of trial by jury with English bills tried by Scottish jurors, and vice versa. This does seem to have been the fairer option as the other methods included trial on the warden's honour and trial by an avower. For the former, the warden had to declare, from his own knowledge and on his honour, whether a complaint against a subject of his own March was valid or not and, if he was mistaken, to take responsibility for the offence himself.

An avower was a fellow countryman of the accused, acceptable to both plaintiff and defendant, who could swear that the case was true.

Although these methods were all open to abuse, justice must have prevailed sometimes otherwise there would have been little point in holding the Day of Truce.

In no way could these 'courts' be said to resemble our modern-day methods of justice. Trials were held out of doors in what was almost a party atmosphere, hardly the setting of a modern courtroom. The accused could be an outlaw or a nobleman, and he could be sure that he was no more guilty than many of the onlookers, or even his accuser. He may even have raided with the judge in a past foray!

The wardens had to strike a balance between the Scots and English when dealing with individual complaints. If equal numbers of bills were to be presented by each side, the wardens had to bargain before the Day of Truce to know which bills would be 'fyled', the total cost, and the total amount of bills 'fyled' to ensure that they were roughly the same.

This balancing act must have resulted in a large number of bills remaining unsettled, often for years. It took William Fenwick of Wallington, for example, six years to get a bill of £30 'fyled' against three of the Robsons.

Even if bills were called, prompt payment was not always forthcoming. A reiver may have been unable or unwilling to offer payment and even when payment was made it was passed from warden to warden and finally to the complainant. It seems unlikely that the right amount would finally be received!

The fact that those accused of crimes may not turn up at the Day of Truce caused many problems. It was the warden's responsibility to see that they did appear, but the lack of prisons, 'nuisance value' of the prisoners, too many prisoners or some that were too influential to arrest, all combined to make this task difficult.

Pledges played an important part in Border life. A pledge was actually a hostage and if, when a bill was 'fyled', the offender could not pay he might be taken as a hostage until the payment was made. In the case of non-appearance of the offender, the warden gave someone else in his place. This may have been one of the warden's officers and, in a somewhat bizarre arrangement, the warden might 'borrow' him back to carry out his duties.

A warden may also offer himself to the opposite side in the event of the death of the accused, or he may even have paid the debt himself in the hope that the dead man's family would pay up.

There were also 'professional' pledges who volunteered themselves in place of the offenders. One member of the Kerr family was a pledge to England for 102 bills. 'Stand-ins' seem to have been readily available, despite the fact that they were likely to be imprisoned in foul conditions. Those from a higher class were kept in private homes and had to pay their own expenses.

The task of the wardens at the Days of Truce was not an easy one: eventually after the bills were 'fyled', fines paid, compromises reached and pledges delivered they had done their best. Business completed, the wardens made a joint proclamation of what had been achieved and a date for the next Day of Truce was agreed. Although they should have been held monthly, the intervals between the Days of Truce increased in later years.

Finally, the wardens and their parties withdrew, the assurance of peace still in force until the following sunrise.

THE RAID OF THE REDESWIRE

"The seventh of July the suith to say,
At the Reidswire the tryst was set;"

❖❖❖❖❖

As mentioned in the previous chapter, the Days of Truce, as well as being official occasions, were also seen as social events where members of the same surname met up and arms were temporarily laid aside.

However, good intentions can sometimes go wrong, and the incident known as the 'Raid of the Redeswire' is one such example.

Alas! That day I'll ne'er forget!
Was sure sae feard, and then sae faine-
They came theare justice for to gett,
Will never green to come again.

Sir John Carmichael, Keeper of Liddlesdale and deputy to the warden William Kerr of Ferniehurst, represented the Scottish side while Sir John Forster, warden of the English Middle March, appeared for the other. Carmichael, a good soldier, was an honest, if blunt man who liked to deal efficiently with the business in hand.

Forster, on the other hand, was something of a rogue, and there were many accusations of misconduct against him and the misuse of his office as warden. He was known to have protected the wild Elliot clan and to have released some thirty Scottish prisoners due to be hung. He also took part in many 'warden rodes' (see page 46) which served to line his personal coffers, as he himself admitted in a letter to Walsingham in 1583, *"it is not the fee of myne office that will maynteyne my house."*

The meeting began normally, as the two cavalcades approached each other and paused to allow the opening ceremony to begin. Most of the company were unarmed and friendly towards each other.

Yet was our meeting meek eneugh,
*Begun wi' merriment and mowes**
*jests

After drinking to each other, the wardens began the business of the day. Everything went well until they reached a bill of complaint against a notorious English thief, named Farnstein. An unlikely name, this was in fact Harry Robson from North Tynedale. Sir John Forster should have produced the prisoner to answer the charge against him, but Robson failed to answer his name, and Forster filed the bill for non-appearance.

Carmichael, however, was unhappy with this, suspecting Sir John of another of his ploys, for which he was famous, and demanded Robson's surrender. Forster promised to produce the offender at the next day of truce but Carmichael refused to continue with the meeting. *"No more can I make further delivery to you, and it appears you cloak justice and are not willing that it should proceed."*

Forster then lost his temper and an argument between the two ensued with Sir John casting aspersions on Carmichael's breeding and his fitness for the warden's duties.

This annoyed the Scottish followers, and Forster, according to the ' Ballad of the Redeswire' :

*Raised and raxed*1 him where he stood*
*And bade him match him with his marrows*2*
And they loot off a flight of arrows.

1* stood up in stirrups 2* companions

The Scots of course argued that the Tynedale men started the fighting with a shout of *"Tot it, Tynedale"*, and proceeded to settle old scores. Once the fracas began, however, the wardens' efforts to put a stop to it failed and the Scots were soon forced to retreat. It was at this point that the cry of *"A Jedworth, a Jedworth"* was heard as the men from Jedburgh, who were late, arrived panting up the hill. A full battle then ensued.

The Tynedale men, quick to take advantage of the situation, plundered the pedlars' stalls as the Scots rode into Redesdale and stole three hundred cattle.

Six Englishmen were killed including Sir George Heron, the deputy warden, and several Englishmen were taken prisoner including Sir Francis Russell, Sir Cuthbert Collingwood, Sir James Ogle, various members of the Fenwick family, and Sir John himself.

To the embarassment of the Regent, Morton, the prisoners were taken to Edinburgh, but as the two countries were not at war, they could not be held, and were returned together with a present of falcons.

Many questions concerning the event were left unanswered. Were the wardens drunk, or was there a private feud between them? Was it the Tynedale men or the Jedburgh men who shot first?

To the annoyance of Queen Elizabeth it was the English who came out of the affair the worst. A meeting of the Border Commissioners was arranged at Berwick but they could not reach any conclusions. It was generally assumed that Carmichael, being relatively new to the Borders had uncovered some of Forster's many dubious activities. Forster, on the other hand, could have been trying to rid himself of the new man by showing him incapable of keeping order.

The incident also severely damaged his own reputation and after being confronted by the Earl of Huntingdon, president of the Council of the North, Forster was said to *"writhe like an eel."* Fortunately the incident, which could have sparked off another Anglo-Scottish war, was allowed to die down quietly.

THE HOT TROD

"Ah! lads, we'll fang them a' in the net!
For I hae a' the fords o' Liddel set."

❖❖❖❖❖

In order to achieve a successful raid across the Border, tactics were an essential part of the reiver's way of life. When planning a foray, the reivers would first rendezvous at a designated place, known to all the members of a particular clan or surname. This would often be marked by a cairn of stones on the moor, and those arriving late would find a mark on the turf or the bark of a tree to show the direction taken by the main raiding party.

The reivers would assemble at these points with their arms and rations and, most importantly, their horses or ponies. The Border reivers way of life depended on the good quality of a mount which could find a safe route through the many bogs and marshes of the Border country. They were also needed to round up the stolen beasts lifted by their lawless masters.

Reiving was mainly a winter occupation when forays could be made under cover of darkness of the long winter nights, and the cattle, standing silently in the moonlight, were strong and healthy.

Those at risk from attack were constantly vigilant, keeping 'Watch and Ward' : i.e. staying awake at night, and looking out in a specific direction during the day. The Border Laws in England laid down which places should be guarded, how and by whom.

They watch, to hear the bloodhound baying:
They watch, to hear the war-horn braying;
To see St. George's red cross streaming;
To see the midnight beacon steaming,
They watch, against Southern force and guile,
Lest Scroop, or Howard, or Percy's powers,
Threaten Branksome's lordly towers,
From Warkworth, or Naworth, or merry Carlisle.

Walter Scott : 'The Lay of the Minstrel'.

The 'Ward' was kept during daylight hours from the hills, where guards could observe tracks and trails normally used by the Border reivers. At night, 'Watch' was kept on the passes and fords from 1st October to 16th March. Any strangers were challenged and, if they had no suitable explanation for out and about, they were taken to be tried before the bailiffs.

If the authorities suspected that a large foray was to be run, they increased the size of the watch from the usual two men to anything up to forty extra guards.

The watcher's task was not any easy one : jumping at every rustle in the undergrowth or ripple of water and, if nothing was heard, the constant fear that they could be attacked at any time.

An early warning system of beacons was also essential for the possible capture of the reivers. These networks were controlled from Carlisle Castle on the English side, and Home Castle on the Scottish side of the Border. The beacons were placed on hillsides, six or seven hundred feet high, and within easy access of the watch man, who, with his horse and cart raced to raise the alarm.

The hill beacons were later supplemented by grates held in heavy stone lanterns displayed on the roof of every tower and castle : *"Everie man that hath a castle or tower of stone shall upon every fray raised in the night give warning to the countries by fire on the topps of the castle tower in such sort as he shall be directed from the warning castle upon paine of 3s.4d."* (about 16 pence.)

Once the alarm was raised, lights would appear across the hills and on the towers, and if the local people were alerted quickly they might possibly meet and repel the raiders. It was more likely, however, that the raid had already quietly taken place, and the victims were left to 'follow their goods.'

Armed, and on horseback, men from neighbouring farms, towers and cottages would join in the legal pursuit of their goods. Each man would carry a smouldering piece of peat, hastily grabbed from the fire, and fanned into flame by the sudden chase. They met their fellow pursuers and raced after the raiders, following the 'hot trod', whereby those who were robbed *"may lawfully follow their goods either with a sleuth hound the trod* (track) *thereof, or else by such other means as they best can devise."*

At first no safe conduct was required when crossing the Border in pursuit of goods, however, later laws required that a man should *"go to any man of good fame and sound judgement, and declaring his cause,"* state which goods had been taken and ask the person to *"witness the trod."*

Although these regulations applied to the wardens also, they were often not adhered to. If a warden was obstructed in any way, the offender was immediately punished, but if the warden or his men caused any unlawful harm, they were handed over to the opposite warden, and often no further action was taken.

The punishment for failing to follow the raiding party had originally been the death penalty, but in 1570 it was reduced to seven days in prison or a fine of 3s 4d. (16 pence.)

A trod led by a warden was likely to be more successful in recovering goods and it was important to ensure that all those following the trod were sympathetic to the capture of the reivers. In 1596 an officer from the English West March led a small trod into Scotland accompanied by ten Grahams and a sleuth hound. They caught up with the raiders, the Kangs - a dangerous branch of the Irvine clan - and the Grahams stood by as the reivers killed the leader, stole his horse and dog and then carried on their way with the stolen goods.

Although the normal practice was to take any captured prisoners either for ransom or to appear before the warden's court, it was not unknown for the reivers to be hanged or lynched on the spot by a trod hungry for revenge.

If for any reason it was not possible to follow the hot trod, there were other ways of recovering one's goods. Firstly, by appealing to the warden within six days of the theft and he would then discuss the matter with his opposite number. Secondly, it was possible to appeal to the opposite warden for a safe conduct to give the victim time to recover his stock or, finally, the 'cold trod', which did not require safe conduct if the pursuer followed within six days of the attack and asked the first 'honest' person he saw across the Border to witness his pursuit.

Although it was illegal to obstruct a man on his 'lawful trod', this did little to prevent him from being ambushed by the reivers.

Even if a trod was successful and the farmer returned home with his beasts, he knew there was little guarantee that the raiders would not strike again.

On April 14th 1597, four Scottish reivers attacked a man's house in the village of Killam, in the English East March, and took off with his cattle. The villagers immediately followed the trod and, catching up with raiders, badly wounded three of them and returned to the village with the men and the stolen cattle. They were to regret allowing the other man to escape.

At dawn forty Scottish raiders arrived in Killam and were fought off by the brave villagers who took two more prisoners. However, the Scots returned within two hours accompanied by one hundred Teviotdale men who proved too much for the villagers, eight of whom were killed, many wounded and the imprisoned reivers were rescued.

The sleuth hounds, the ancestors of the modern bloodhound, and so called because of their ability to follow a slot or trail, played an important part in the capture of the reivers. They were particularly effective if the raiders were driving slow beasts such as pigs, and were unable to make a swift escape. Without the dogs' help it would have been almost impossible to pick up the 'trod' or to find a track through the moorland at night.

There were two ways in which the reivers could throw off the dogs. They could slaughter one of the stolen beasts, hoping the hounds would stop to eat the carcass, or attempt to destroy the scent by riding through rivers and burns.

"By wily turns, by desperate bounds,
Had baffled Percy's best blood-hounds."

So vital were these dogs in the recovery of stolen goods, that they often changed hands for the huge amount of £25 sterling. The English wardens kept a 'calendar' to show where every slue dog was to be found within their area, and the regulations of the Barony of Gilsland included a requirement for each tenant to keep a hound. Even after the Union of the Crowns, the dogs were kept at designated places and used to track cattle thieves.

THE DEBATEABLE LAND

"There is a grounde called the Debateable Grounde, lyeing betwene the realme of England and Scotland, where in there is no strife for the boundes of the same."

The Debateable Land, so called because of a dispute over ownership, was a narrow strip of Border country about four miles wide and over twelve miles long. It was bounded to the east by the River Esk and in the west by the River Sark, with Tarras Moss to the north.

For such a small area of land, it was the cause of considerable aggravation. Neither the Scots or the English would admit to ownership and so neither could be held responsible for what took place. The result was that both English and Scottish outlaws and troublemakers gathered *"delighting in all mischief, and most unnaturally and cruelly wasting and destroying, harrying and slaying, their own neighbours."*

Periodically the authorities would devastate the land, clearing all the buildings and making it unfit for habitation. The type of rogues who lived there, however, were not easily discouraged and they soon returned and continued to raid into both countries. The estates of many of the Grahams were in the Debateable Land, together with some Armstrongs and Bells.

Efforts were made to 'improve' the area : the English and Scottish wardens proposed to compile lists of the other's subjects who were hiding there, to surrender them and start all over again. However, it was difficult to assert authority and the situation continued whereby the rogues raided at will into either kingdom. If either country put pressure on them, they threatened to go over to the other side, playing one against the other.

Finally, Lord Dacre, warden of the English West March, decided that enough was enough. Ill Wills Sandy, an Armstrong with a particularly bad reputation, had been in the pay of England, but now complained against Lord Maxwell, the Scottish warden, saying he was causing problems for him and his grayne. The Grahams, supposedly English, also became indignant and all threatened to go over to the Scots if matters were not put right.

Lord Dacre was furious at the implications of blackmail, especially on a warden, and approached the Scottish authorities to put an end to it once and for all. He had already made various sorties into the Debateable Lands against the Armstrongs. At one time he secretly assembled two thousand riders and hoped to surprise and capture Johnny Armstrong and Sim the Laird. The English Storeys, however, warned the Armstrongs and Dacre's men were forced back, badly injured. He soon returned, now armed with artillery, and was successful in destroying Hollows Tower, home of Johnny Armstrong. Armstrong too, was out raiding that day and he destroyed Netherby and a mill belonging to Lord Dacre at Gilsland.

War now raged between Dacre and the inhabitants of the Debateable Land and he invaded again in March 1528, destroying many strongholds, including Ill Will Armstrong's tower.

The Scots were agreeable to Dacre's proposals that something must be done to solve the problem and in 1551 a joint commission sat to consider constructing a march dyke. An earthwork was subsequently built which ran from the Esk, just below its junction with Liddel Water, to the Sark, which it followed to the Solway.

Very little remains of the dyke today, each end was originally marked by a square stone bearing the arms of the respective countries. The wardens had hoped for an end to the trouble, but it was not to be. The Debateable Lands still attracted all kinds of low life, although now the Border Law could be enforced as the wardens knew the extent of their jurisdiction.

"At the sacred font, the priest
Through ages left the master hand unblest
To urge with keener airm the blood encrusted spear."
Leyton.

❖❖❖❖❖

'Deadly Feud' was the conflict between the different clans and was at the root of many of the Border problems. If a man was slain, for whatever reason, it was the duty, handed down from father to son, of his nearest kin to avenge him. The death which started off the feud could have taken place during a foray or it could have been in single combat, possibly as a result of 'bauchling' (see Border Laws page 14) to settle a matter of honour.

Once the feud started it could last for ever as each clan retaliated against the other. Every member of the grayne was involved and no juryman who passed the death sentence, no one defending his life or property was safe from revenge on himself, his family, or surname.

Revenge was so much a part of the Borderers' way of life, that the church was even forced to recognise it. At a baptism the right hand of a male child was left unchristened so that *"it might deal the more deadly, in fact the more hallowed, blow to the enemy."* (Walter Scott)

The feuds could amount to civil wars or could be solved by single combat, even the wardens could find themselves at feud. They were usually between Scot and Scot, or English and English, and the clans could be involved with several at the same time.

One famous Border feud, between the Scotts of Buccleuch and the Kers of Cessford, festered for most of the sixteenth century. In 1526 the Laird of Buccleuch ('Wicked Wat') decided to rescue the young James V from the clutches of the Earl of Angus. When James planned to visit the Border, Buccleuch asked him to stay at Branxholm. Angus, however, would not fall for such a plot and the only alternative was to ambush him at the Bridge of Melrose.

Buccleuch had gathered together an army of almost a thousand Scotts, Elliots and Armstrongs and the ambush soon developed into what became known as the Battle of Darnick.

Buccleuch's men held out against the Angus clan, supported by Homes and Kers, but as often happened the army gradually dispersed, due to ties of marriage and mutual dislike etc., leaving Buccleuch to escape. As the Elliots set off to Liddlesdale with the Kers in pursuit, Sir Andrew Ker of Cessford was killed by one of the Elliots at a place called Turnagain. As a result of this incident, Buccleuch had to flee to France but was later pardoned and he returned to his estates. Elliot was not as fortunate, as he was arrested and taken to Edinburgh to be hanged.

This was just the start of the feud and over the years several evil deeds were carried out in the name of family honour. One particularly bad incident took place a generation later in Edinburgh's High Street where a group of Kers and their friends, including some Homes, encountered Wicked Wat. In the inevitable confrontation which followed young Ker of Cessford held back but Home of Coldenknowes ran Scott through with his weapon, crying to Ker : *"Strike, traitor, a stroke for thy father's sake."* After this, not surprisingly, the Scotts were not inclined to turn the other cheek.

The Kers were not the only grayne with whom the Scotts remained in deadly feud. In 1564 the Elliots conducted a raid into Teviotdale, murdering a number of people. Retaliation in kind from the Scotts resulted in a mayhem which rattled the Border. Official retribution, for once, took over swiftly. Five of the main offenders from each clan were captured and taken to Edinburgh, tried, and beheaded on Castle Hill.

The Elliots, however, were not to be cheated and they invaded Buccleuch's estates burning and pillaging for ten miles around, with no mercy for man, woman or child. Buccleuch made a demand to the Queen for permission to avenge the slaughter. Knowing the answer would most certainly be in the negative, he rode into Liddlesdale where he and his men killed seven Elliots and Croziers, together with their allies, and then returned with as many cattle as they could drive.

One particularly fierce surname were the Tweedys, whose chief was the Laird of Drumelzier, near Peebles. They carried on a vicious feud with their neighbours, the Veitches. *"Wherever a Veitch and a Tweedy met, they fought, and fought to kill."* In 1590 their quarrel reached a climax. Deil O'Dowyck, the chief of the Veitches, had been continually harassing the Tweedys, assisted by a Burnet, known as the 'Hoolet of Barns', because of his nocturnal activities.

One day as the Deil's son rode into Peebles, he was ambushed opposite Neidpath Castle by nine of the Tweedys who were lying in wait for him. *"It was no fight, but bloody murder."* Recrimination swiftly followed as the Veitches laid an ambush for John Tweedy and murdered him.

As one of the aspects of deadly feud was the effects of intermarriage between one clan and another, the Tweedy's revenge was against James Geddes, Dawyck's brother-in-law. They lay in wait for him in the Kirk Wynd in Edinburgh and *"Rushit out of the said close and shots of pistolets slew him behind his back."*

There was also much rivalry between the Maxwells and the Johnstones, two great Dumfriesshire surnames. They carried out few raids against the English as the rivalry between the two chiefs occupied most of their time. This was made worse by the fact that kings and regents rewarded each in turn with the wardenry of the Scottish West March, much to the aggravation of the other.

When James Douglas, Earl of Morton, was executed in 1581, Lord John Maxwell at last inherited the earldom and estates he had coveted for so long. Instead of being grateful for his good fortune, he put the earldom at risk by using the power it gave him to the benefit of himself and his grayne, rather than to try and keep order.

Ignoring his obligation as warden he put together an army of his own household and tenants, and a motley crew of Armstrongs and Grahams, and proceeded to raid Ettrick Forest. He captured Adam Scott and Thomas Dalgleish, holding them for a huge ransom.

Morton was asked to appear before the Privy Council as a result of his behaviour, but he refused and a Johnstone was made warden in his place. Johnstone of Dunskellie, the new warden, was told to take Maxwell into custody and troops were sent from

Edinburgh to help him in his task. However, they were attacked at Crawfordmuir by Robert Maxwell, the chief's half-brother.

Now the battle really began!

Robert Maxwell burned Johnstone's castle of Lochwood and then the clan proceeded to raid, burning 300 houses and taking 3,000 sheep and cattle belonging to the Johnstones.

The Johnstones waited until spring when they attacked Dumfries twice but were beaten by the weather. Once again Maxwell retaliated and raided the Johnstones until finally Johnstone died and the King faced the task of finding a new warden. He took the only option available and appointed a Maxwell on condition that the graynes would call a truce.

This was not to last, however, and it was the Johnstones who broke it. William Johnstone of Wamphray, 'The Galliard', attacked the Maxwell allies, the Crichtons, who in turn caught Johnstone and hung him.

Revenge was swift as the Johnstones devasted Nithsdale, the area inhabited by the Maxwells. Defence was weak and many people suffered. A deputation of women travelled to Edinburgh to seek redress for their murdered husbands, taking with them their blood-soaked shirts. Their protest was ignored so they demonstrated in Edinburgh's streets, brandishing the gory shirts until the King was forced to act. He ordered the warden (Maxwell) to arrest Johnstone of Dunskellie and if he refused to surrender, he was to attack his castle and *"raze out the memory of him and his name in these bounds."* Taking a thousand men with him, Maxwell found the Johnstones lined up ready for what was to become known as the Battle of Dryfe Sands.

During the battle Maxwell was knocked from his horse, and being tall and weighed down with armour, he was left for dead. There are different versions of what happened next. One relates that the Galliard's nephew, Willy Johnstone, killed Maxwell and cut off his arm. Another states that Willy mutilated Maxwell but he was actually killed by the wife of Johnstone of Kirkhill with a blow from the tower keys which hung from her waist. Whatever took place, Maxwell's arm was taken as a trophy and nailed to the wall at Lochwood.

After the battle the feud dragged on for another fifteen years until the then Lord Maxwell suggested a friendly meeting between himself and the chief of the Johnstones, each to be accompanied by one attendant. This was not as innocent as it seemed. Maxwell had previously arranged that his attendant should quarrel with his opposite number and shoot him dead. After this, Maxwell shot Johnstone twice in the back, killing him.

As a result of his appalling behaviour Maxwell had to leave the country for France where he stayed for four years, showing little remorse. Justice did triumph in the end as Maxwell was betrayed on his return to Scotland and subsequently executed.

Other families in 'deadly feud' included the Collingwoods against the Selbys, the Greys against Widdringtons, Scotts against Charltons and Elliots against Charltons.

The Privy Council of Scotland tried several times to put an end to particular feuds. Eventually in 1600, an Arbitration Act was passed which required those involved to *"submit to two or three friends on either side"* who should meet within thirty days to make a reconciliation or to appoint an 'overman' to decide the case. The authorities naively believed that if those involved in a feud swore not to harm each other, their relations or friends, then peace would come about.

Another way of settling feuds was to bring the dispute before the courts to agree compensation for lives lost. Success was unlikely as there were problems in proving who was at fault. An alternative was to settle out of court, but this depended on the 'promises' of those involved!

While it was not easy to bring an end to a feud within one territory, it was much more difficult to stop when both countries were involved. At one time Sir John Forster reported that there were twenty four Northumberland surnames at feud with ten in Scotland. On occasions, revenge on a large scale could virtually wipe out a small grayne.

Taking into account the conditions of the time and the Borderer's way of life, perhaps it is not surprisingly that 'Deadly Feud' became an almost acceptable part of the reivers existence.

THE ARMSTRONGS

"On the Border was the Armstrongs, ablemen,
Somewhat unruly, and very ill to tame."
Satchells.

Probably the most feared and dangerous clan, the Armstrongs were mainly Scottish and inhabited Liddlesdale, Eskdale, Annandale, the Scottish West March and English Middle March, as well as the Debateable Land (see page 30). At the beginning of the sixteenth century they could easily gather together three thousand men for a raiding party and they were perhaps the most successful at plundering the English countryside. The Armstrongs often inter-married with English surnames which meant they could count on support when raiding into Cumberland and Tynedale.

Some of the more famous Border characters were Armstrongs, including Johnnie Armstrong, Kinmont Willie, Ill Will Armstrong and Jock of the Side.

Johnny Armstrong of Gilnockie, a distant relative of Kinmont Willie, and the brother of Mangerton, chief of the Armstrongs, was one of the most notorious of the Border reivers and his name has passed into our northern folklore. His headquarters, at Gilnockie Tower, overlooked the River Esk, near Canonbie. Although, according to legend, Hollows Tower was said to be his home, it was in fact, a half a mile away.

During the early sixteenth century Henry VIII encouraged the Scots and English to continue their feud, supporting his wardens in their complaints against the Scots which could then result in English reprisals. By 1529, the Borders were in constant ferment as robbery, murder and arson became a way of life.

The young King James, then about seventeen years old, was determined to calm the situation, feeling that he could create peace. It was during one of the king's descents upon the Border that the events occurred which finally resulted in Johnny

Armstrong's execution.

Having dealt severely with various lairds along the Scottish border, the king felt in need of relaxation and the Earls of Huntly, Argyll and Athol were summoned to hunt deer with him. The bag came to 360 and, spurred on by his success, James declared an amnesty inviting Gilnockie to take part in the chase.

Johnny and his men, dressed in their Sunday best, rode to join the royal party, but on the journey they were stopped and brought before the king, not as guests, but under guard. James appears to have been annoyed by Johnny's finery - not suitable, he thought, for a common criminal.

There hang nine targets at Johnnie's hat,*
And ilk ane worth three hundred pound.
What wants that knave that a king should have,
But the sword of honour and the crown?

John wore a girdle about his middle,
Imbroidered ower wi' burning gold,
Bespangled wi' the same metal;
Maist beautiful was to behold.

* tassels

Angry words ensued, resulting in the order that Armstrong and his followers were to be hanged.

Three days after these events Gilnockie's estates were given to Maxwell, which raises the point that it was Maxwell who issued the invitation in the king's name, without his knowledge, and that the whole incident was a carefully planned trap.

It is also possible that no harm was intended to Johnny, but that the king's guard seeing a strong armed body of men, had no choice but to escort them to the king. Armstrong no doubt, as was common with so many reivers, had a high opinion of himself and his manner infuriated the king.

Once the king had made his intention clear, Johnny employed 'a silver tongue' to talk himself out of the situation, another reiver trait. The king, however, was not to be moved:

"Away, away, thou traitor strang!
Out o' my sight soon may'st thou be!
I grantit nevor a traitor's life,
And now I'll not begin with w' thee."

Johnny tried again, stating that he never robbed his fellow Scots, only the 'auld enemy'. This only incensed the king more as he was not at war with England and resented his subjects attacking the English. Johnny's last plea to include the king in his protection racket across the Border was the final straw.

"Grant me my life, my liege, my king!
And a brave gift I'll gie to thee-
All between here and Newcastle town
Sall pay their yeirly rent to thee."

Finally, Johnny had to admit defeat:

"To seek het water beneith cauld ice,
Surely it is a great folie-
I have asked grace at a graceless face,
But there is nane for my men and me."

Armstrong and his men were hanged, twelve in Edinburgh and the rest at Carlenrig, ten miles along the road from Hawick to Langholm.

John was murdered at Carlinrigg,
And all his gallant cumpanie;
But Scotland's heart was ne'er sae wae,
To see sae mony brave men die-

It is here in the old churchyard that Johnny Armstrong and his men lie, and it is possible to make out the name of 'John Armstrong of Gilnockie' on one of the old weathered tombstones.

Will Armstrong, known as Kinmont Willie, one of the most famous of the Border Reivers, was born around 1530, the grandson of Ill Wills Sandy. He normally lived at Woodhouselee, on the River Esk, and was related to the nearby Graham clan through marriage to Hutchen Graham's daughter. His own daughter later became the wife of Thomas Carleton of Gilsland, giving him 'a foot in both camps.'

Like his grandfather before him, Kinmont gathered around him some of the worst villains, known as 'Kinmont's Bairns.' This lawless bunch, as many as 300, raided on a large scale and usually rode by day from Kinmont's tower at Morton Rigg, just north of Carlisle. They raided deep into the English countryside, in Northumberland and Cumberland, as well as harassing those on their own side of the Border.

Their favourite target, however, was Tynedale and in August 1583, during a raid against the Milburns, 8 villages were attacked, houses burned, 800 cattle stolen, £200 worth of goods taken, 6 men killed and 11 wounded, and 30 prisoners taken.

The following year, 1584, together with Nebless Clem Croser and 300 men, he stole 1300 cattle, 60 horses and £2,000 worth of goods. His largest raid took place in 1593 when he ran a foray into Tynedale with 1,000 men stealing 2,000 beasts and £330 worth of goods.

Henry, Lord Scrope, warden of the English West March regarded Kinmont as his own personal enemy and was determined to capture him. In 1593, Thomas, Lord Scrope, succeeded his father and he was just as intent on capturing the notorious Kinmont Willie. Scrope had antagonised Sir Walter Scott of Buccleuch, recently appointed Keeper of Liddlesdale, by appealing directly to King James of Scotland for help in controlling Kinmont Willie. Buccleuch objected strongly to this and a clash between the two was inevitable.

On 17th March, 1596, a day of truce was held between Mr. Scott for the Scottish West March, and Mr. Salkeld for the English. It started as a routine affair, attended by Kinmont Willie who assumed himself safe from arrest during the amnesty.

After the meeting, Kinmont rode home with the deputy,

Scott, until they parted and the outlaw continued with three or four friends to Woodhouselee. Salkeld also returned home, riding along the English side of the river with about 200 men. Just before the junction of the Liddle and the Esk, the English forded the river and captured Kinmont Willie:

They band his legs beneath the steed
They tied his hands behind his back!
They guarded him, fivesome on each side,
And they brought him ower the Liddle-rack.

Thus bound, they escorted Kinmont to Carlisle Castle.

That this should happen on a day of truce caused uproar throughout the Borders. Scrope argued that the period of truce ended at sunset, but this meant that anyone riding a short distance home could be captured, a risk the Border Law sought to prevent. However, now that he had his sworn enemy in gaol, Scrope was not going to miss the opportunity to dispense with him once and for all.

Buccleuch saw the incident as an infringement of his powers and, after complaining to the necessary officials without success, took the law into his own hands and planned to rescue Kinmont Willie.

And have they e'en ta'en him, Kinmont Willie,
Against the truce of Border tide?
And forgotten that the bauld Buccleuch
Is Keeper here on the Scottish side?

Spies on the English side of the Border reported that Carlisle Castle was 'surpriseable.' Fearing that a delay could result in Kinmont's hanging, Buccleuch gathered together Armstrongs, Scotts, Elliots and Grahams, three Walter Scotts, including Wat o' Harden and the chief of the Armstrongs, Mangerton.

On a dark rainy night, the 13th April, 1596, 200 reivers gathered about ten miles from Carlisle, equipped with ladders and weapons to force the walls and gates of its castle.

And five and five, like a mason gang
That carried the ladders lang and hie;
And five and five, like broken men,
And so they reach'd the Woodhouselee.

With dawn only two hours away, the men reached the River Eden below Carlisle Castle. The night was pitch black, as torrents of rain soaked the men and, to add to the terrible conditions, the river was shrouded in mist. Risking their lives, they swam their horses loaded with equipment, across the raging river and landed on the flat ground to the north of the castle, known as Sauceries Flat. (*now a public park)*

The spies in the castle, however, had miscalculated the length of the ladders required to reach the top of the castle wall. Fortunately, the rescuers located a small oak postern, or door, still to be seen to the west of the castle.

Many of the guards were either asleep or taking shelter from the torrential rain, and the rescue proved relatively easy. Breaking through the postern, Buccleuch and two dozen men made for the part of the castle in which Kinmont was detained. While the rescue was taking place, the other raiders made as much noise as possible in the hope that the guards might over estimate their numbers.

"Now sound out trumpets!" quo' Buccleuch;
"Let's waken Lord Scroope right merrilie!"-

Very few guards attempted to repel the reivers until after the rallying call signifying a successful operation - 'the old arrogant slogan of the Elliots'-

Then loud the warden's trumpet blew-
"O wha dare meddle wi' me?"

Scarcely had Buccleuch and his men left the castle when the garrison pulled itself together:

We scarce had won the Staneshaw bank,
When a' the Carlisle bells were rung,
And a thousand men on horse and foot,
Cam wi' the keen Lord Scroope along.

The high torrents of the river, however, prevented Scrope's men from following, and as the lord himself observed concerning Buccleuch:

"He is either himsel' a devil from hell,
Or else his mother a witch maun be,
I wadna' have ridden that wan water
For a' the gawd in Christentie."

Scrope ordered an immediate enquiry as his enemies revelled in his failure, and his superiors demanded an explanation as to how Carlisle Castle had been so easily breached. The two wardens who had previously worked against a common enemy, now lost faith in each other's good will. Criticism of his actions, ensured that Scrope was even more determined to repress the reivers.

After this dramatic episode Kinmont was involved in relatively minor forays and he now had joint command of a gang known as 'Sandys Bairns.' He attacked the village of Scotby in 1600 with 140 riders, burning, taking prisoners and over 100 cattle. Later that day, showing some of his old sparkle, he and his men rode into Carlisle and smashed doors in Rickergate, damaged the bridge chains, captured some prisoners and rode under the castle wall shouting *"Upon them, upon them, a Dacre, a Dacre, a red bull, a red bull!"* The inhabitants raised the alarm but the raiders soon left to sober up!

The following year he operated a protection racket at Scaleby, receiving stolen goods and dealing in illicit horse trading. He carried out his last raid in 1602 and was still alive two years later. It seems as if the old rogue probably died in his own bed!

He is weil kend, John of the Syde
A greater thief did never ride.
He never tyris[1]
For to brek byris.[2]

[1]tires [2]break byres

Jock o' the Side's claim to fame was largely as a result of his daring escape from Newcastle, recalled in the famous ballad. John Armstrong, a nephew of Mangerton, Chief of the Armstrongs, had his headquarters at the Side, a tower in Liddlesdale, on the west bank of Liddel Water.

In 1527 Armstrong found himself imprisoned at Newcastle along with *"divers thieves of Scotland and traitors of Tynedale."*

Now Liddlesdale has ridden a raid,
But I wat they had better staid at hame;
For Michael o' Wingfield he is dead,
And Jock o' Side is prisoner ta'n.

His uncle, Mangerton, swore to rescue his nephew and set out from Liddlesdale.

Three men I'll send to set him free,
Weel harnessed a wi' best o' steel;
The English rogues may hear, and drie
The weight o' their braid-swords to feel.

The Laird's Jock ane, the Laird's Wat* twa,*
O, Hobbie Noble thou ane mawn be!*
Thy coat is blue, thou hast been true,
Since England banished thee to me!

(*The Laird's Jock and the Laird's Wat were Mangerton's sons, but it is unlikely that Hobbie Noble, an outlaw from Bewcastle, was actually in the party.)

With little time to waste, as Jock could have been hanged without a trial, the group, disguised as merchants, crossed the

Tyne at Chollerford and made a ladder from a tree which they had cut down. With the help of Sir William Lisle and his son they rescued the prisoner, despite the fact that the ladder was too short! It appears from the ballad that Jock had to ride side saddle as he was weighed down with *"full fifteen stane o' Spanish iron."*

O, Jock, sae winsomely's ye ride,
Wi' baith feet upon ae side,
Sae weel ye're hariest, and sae trig,*
In troth ye sit like ony bride.

*neat

Arriving again at Chollerford, they found the Tyne in full spate and discussed among themselves the next move:

Then out and spak the Laird's saft Wat,
The greatest coward on the cumpanie,
"Now halt, now halt! We need na' try't;
The day is come we a' maun die."

The Laird's Wat could well have been afraid of braving the flood, with Jock wearing that weight of iron, however it seems they did reach Liddlesdale safely and survived to fight another day!

Sae now they're away for Liddlesdale,
E'en as fast as they could them, hie;
The prisoner is brought to's ain fireside,
And there o's airns they mak him free.*

*of the irons

'WARDEN RODES'

"And by my faith," the gateward said,
"I think 'twill prove a Warden Raid."
Walter Scott : 'The Lay of the Last Minstrel'

From time to time, when the usual forces of law had failed, it was a warden's duty to carry out peace-time raids (or 'rodes') across the Border. This duty was often abused and raids were carried out just for the sake of it, making it hard to distinguish between these and the official 'Warden Rodes'.

A warden raid was different from a campaign ordered by the sovereign. Several battles of this nature took place during Henry VIII's reign when national generals took command and the two countries were officially 'at war'. After the Scots had made a number of raids as a result of bad treatment at the hands of the English, Henry finally lost patience and let it be known that retaliation was acceptable: the philosophy of 'an eye for an eye, a tooth for a tooth' came into force. In 1532, for example, the Earl of Northumberland plundered the Scottish Middle March and Buccleuch, Cessford and Ferniehurst joined forces to retaliate.

There were three main reasons why a warden might wish to carry out a raid. Firstly, it was sometimes difficult to bring to justice an offender whose surname persistently sheltered him. As an individual punishment proved impossible, it was often thought prudent that all the surname should suffer for the guilt of one.

Secondly, the warden had the right to pursue the goods stolen from a victim of a Border raid, even if it meant crossing the frontier.

Finally, the actions of a particular grayne may have been so despicable as to warrant a full expedition *"accompanied by the entire force of the wardenry and with displayed banners"*, to lay waste the entire area by sword and fire.

To avoid misuse of this right, the Treaty of 1484 stated that a 'rode' should not be entered into without permission from a higher authority. It was impossible to follow this to the letter as immediate pursuit was often necessary if there was to be any hope of success, particularly when goods had been stolen.

Occasionally it was necessary to conduct an extended rode. In Scotland this would be led by the king, but in England the warden, or someone on his behalf, would lead it. Thomas Carlton, for example, made a lengthy visit into Dumfriesshire and captured the Johnstone stronghold of Lochwood. The longest, and best executed rode, however, was probably that led by Sir Robert Carey into Liddlesdale.

The Armstrongs had just carried out a large scale attack on Haltwhistle and Carey was determined to stamp on the lawless raiders. Having recently taken over as warden of the English Middle March, he was offered a hundred soldiers for his warden's force, but he accepted only forty. With these men, his deputies Sir Henry Widdrington and Sir William Fenwick, and about another 150 other volunteers, Carey set out for Liddlesdale.

The Armstrongs had retreated with their families, goods and animals as they usually did after stirring up trouble, to Tarras Moss - *"a large and great forest...surrounded by bog and marsh"* - through which only they knew the paths. As it was the middle of June, the Armstrongs were quite happy to stay there all summer with plenty of grazing for the animals and wood to build shelters.

From this safe haven they sent provocative messages to Carey saying he had their permission to visit them, weather permitting! They also compared Sir Robert to the 'puff of the haggis': hot first but soon to cool off.

Carey, however, was content to wait and, as he wrote in his memoirs: *"By the help of the foot of Redesdale and Tynedale, we had soon built a pretty fort and, within it we had all cabins made to lie on."* He placed a watch on the English side of the Moss and sent 150 men to the other side where the terrain was easier. Using this strategy, Carey succeeded in ousting the Armstrongs from their retreat, captured five important members of the family, as well as taking sheep and cattle.

Not wishing to lose face, the Armstrongs spread a story, the truth of which is debateable, that while Carey was in Liddlesdale they had, in fact, been raiding his lands. They claimed to have sent him part of one of his own cows in case he was short of rations!

The wardens had three different forces at their disposal to help in their raids. Firstly, the law demanded that every able-bodied man from the Border counties should bear arms and turn up when needed to repel an invasion or help the warden when required. To this end comprehensive registers, or muster-rolls, were kept in England showing, by towns, the numbers available, sometimes by name, and whether they were foot soldiers - 'able' or, 'able in horse and harness' - soldiers on horseback.

Muster days were held from time to time and as most of the male population were available for service, these usually became public holidays. The muster rolls also listed the weapons which each man owned. These varied considerably, for example, in a muster of the English East March in 1584 the majority were armed only with a spear, few of them owning bows.

Many of the men would also have jacks and a steel bonnet which provided basic protection, as well as arm and shoulder armour and a gorget which covered the throat. Horsemen as well as wearing body armour, carried a shield and were armed with swords, daggers and pistols.

The second source of a warden's force was his own personal bodyguard and those soldiers who formed the garrisons which were placed at strategic points, such as Chipchase Castle, Bewcastle and Norham. Reinforcements could also be requested from the garrison at Berwick. Garrisons on the Scottish side of the Border included the castles of Hermitage, Home and Lochmaben, in Dumfriesshire.

Finally, mercenaries might be used. They were mainly French on the Scottish side and Italian, Spanish or German on the English side of the frontier.

The men who took part in the warden rodes found themselves unpopular with their fellow Borderers as one of the main points of a raid was the burning of houses and crops stored for food. While the houses could easily be rebuilt, the loss of the crops had wider implications - how were the people to be fed? Even the loss of cattle was not disastrous, as these could be replaced by stealing from another herd.

Pursuing goods immediately after the crime was committed was one thing, but to go out 'cold' to menace people who could well be related through marriage and whose way of life was similar to one's own, was difficult for the locally recruited men.

Even the professional soldiers dreaded such a raid as the paths to the reivers hideouts, through forest and bog, were almost impossible to detect. There was always the risk of ambush and finding themselves floundering, or even drowning, in a filthy swamp as the 'enemy' rode on by.

Scottish kings often took matters into their hands and approached the Border bent on retribution. The expedition of James V which ended in the execution of Johnny Armstrong (see page 37) was a fine example. The young king, only seven and somewhat naive, thought he could bring peace to the Borders. He intended to *"gar the rush bush, keep the cow"*, which, translated, meant that he would create such peace on the Borders that only brushwood, rather than force, would be needed to keep a man's cattle from straying.

Unfortunately the English king, Henry VIII, was determined to nurture disruption and disorder on the Border to the extent of encouraging his wardens to make up complaints against the Scots and to carry out 'rodes' in retribution.

These actions were so successful that by 1529 the Borders were in chaos as robbery and murder became a way of life. James and his advisers decided that the time had come to strike. Firstly, he attacked the Earl of Bothwell, seized his lands and imprisoned the Earl at Edinburgh Castle. The Lords Home and Maxwell, the lairds of Buccleuch, Ferniehurst, Polwarth and Johnstone were also taken prisoner and other families had to give hostages as to their good behaviour.

Others, however, were not as fortunate. James caught Cockburn of Henderland on Meggat Water and accused him not only of theft, but of conspiring with Henry and the Earl of Angus against him and the Scottish throne. Adam Scott of Tushielaw, the 'King of Thieves', was caught in Ettrick and charged with a variety of crimes, in particular he was accused of *"theftuously taking*

Blackmail." Tradition says that these two were both taken from their homes and hanged, Cockburn over his own gate and Scott from the nearest tree. In reality, they were taken to Edinburgh and tried and, according to Bishop Leslie *"convict thair for and heidit* (beheaded), *and their heidis* (heads) *fixit upon the Tolbuith of Edinburg."*

James then went on to lay the trap for Johnnie Armstrong, as previously mentioned. Conditions on the Border did not improve as James had hoped and all loyalty to the crown finally dwindled away.

Many of the Armstrongs simply moved to Cumberland and, spurred on by the treatment they had received, carried on their reiving with a vengeance!

In reality it seems that the 'Warden Rode' was an excuse for 'legalised' pillage and plunder, showing the wardens as little better than those they pursued with such intensity.

UNION OF THE CROWNS

"But since King James the Sixth to England went,
There's been no course of grief or discount."

❖❖❖❖❖

The death of Elizabeth I and the succession of James VI of Scotland to James I of a United Kingdom, saw an end to the reivers heyday. Many felt that the Union of the Crowns had come just in time as the disorder and chaos on the Border had reached such a pitch that the authorities were at a loss as to how to deal with it.

The reivers saw the period between Elizabeth's death and the proclamation of a successor as a period when peace was suspended and they were determined to 'make hay while the sun shone.' This period became known as 'Ill Week' as the Grahams, Armstrongs, Elliots and others joined together for one last foray across the Border. They went as far south as Penrith and made off with 1,280 cattle and 3,801 sheep and goats.

Shortly after his succession James dismissed the idea of separate Marches and abolished the post of warden : if the frontier no longer existed there was no reason to guard it. He then set about bringing peace to the area, firstly taking a psychological approach by changing the name to the Middle Shires. Secondly, on a more practical note, he set up a commission to administer the law. The Border Laws were abolished and although these had been subject to abuse, they were more acceptable than the ordinary law of the land.

James was determined that the lawless raiders should submit to the law and discipline of the rest of Britain. This was a tall order - to sweep aside a whole way of life led by people who believed the only way to survive was by plunder and pillage. The reivers normal methods of resistance which had been successful for generations no longer worked now that the two countries were one. They had lost their great advantage of playing one side off against the other.

The law, however, was adamant - anyone who did not conform faced the gallows or exile.

In the first year of the union 32 Elliots, Armstrongs, Johnstones and others were hung, 15 banished and 140 outlawed.

Walter Scott of Buccleuch, once a notorious reiver himself, was instrumental in bringing calm to the Borders. In 1603 around 2,000 Scots served under Buccleuch as mercenaries and travelled to the Low Countries to aid them in their war against the Spanish.

The Grahams were singled out for persecution as they had played one side against the other to the extent that everyone was opposed to them. Their lands were confiscated on April 17th, 1605 and they were listed to be sent to garrisons in the Low Countries. The government had promised to find homes for the exiles but failed, and the Grahams gradually began to drift back to Eskdale and other areas on the Border. As a result of signing a document produced by the Commissioners the whole surname, women and children included, were banished to Ireland: *"We therefore pray that we may be relegated and banished as an evil colony to some other part of the kingdom, there to spend the remains of our lives in sorrow, for our offence."* It was, indeed, an extraordinary document for the Grahams to agree to!

The Armstrongs too went to Ireland, where a plan had been formulated for the voluntary settlement of Ulster to support the Protestant population. Those who came back to the Borders found that their lands had been given to the Scotts and Elliots.

Of the remaining outlaws, 120 were sent to fight in Bohemia while a further 320 from Tynedale served in Ireland.

Gradually then the old reiving way of life disappeared. Violence still continued on the frontier and bands of mosstroopers appeared in the 17th century, but these could not be regarded in the same light as the reivers. The name 'mosstrooper' was derived quite simply from the fact that the raiders operated in the mossy, peat bog area of the Middle and West areas of the Border, and rode together in troops.

It has been suggested that the mosstroopers were simply reduced groups of Border reivers who had survived the pacification period. However, they were operating in a different climate with a new kind of landlord control and a better legal system. The mosstrooper was a fairly inconspicuous figure, although armed with a pistol and sword, he wore no body armour or steel helmet. They were not as violent as the reivers, probably because many of the traditions such as Deadly Feud, 'bauchling' and other acts of revenge were no longer in evidence.

Not all the family names were extinguished after the Union of the Crowns and there were still Armstrongs, Elliots and Grahams around in the Debateable Lands. The Rakkes (a branch of the Armstrongs) were one of the most prominent families whose members were mosstroopers They lived in Liddlesdale at the Hillhouse, about a mile from the Border. In 1640 the family included Hob Rakkes and his three sons, George or Geordie, Hob and Sym. Geordie was well-known as a mosstrooper and in April 1640 he and ten others, including more Armstrongs, Hendersons and Elliots raided in the South Tyne valley, stealing 80 cows and oxen belonging to Roger Harbottle and his tenants.

Once a theft had been committed, the culprit was immediately followed by the victims involved, occasionally accompanied by a slew hound, similar to the 'Hot Trod'. Often goods could be recovered through negotiation and compensation might be paid. The beasts might be hidden and then sold on: an owner could sometimes be forced to buy back his own animals!

As far as capturing the mosstroopers and bringing them to justice was concerned, there were several weaknesses in the system. A list was drawn up in 1641, for example, of the law breakers which included many Armstrongs and Grahams. In 1643 courts were set up at Jedburgh and Dumfries to deal with a long list of offenders, and on 1st April 1645 the Scottish Privy Council commissioned the Earls of Annandale and Buccleuch to take action against the mosstroopers.

On 15th January, 1645, the Grand Jury of Northumberland at Alnwick claimed that 200 offenders had been caught and imprisoned, but they expressed concern at the numbers still in hiding.

By 1651 the name 'mosstrooper' was applied to any law breaker in the Border area including murderers and highwaymen.

The exception was in Liddlesdale and the Debateable Lands where there was little administrative control and the mosstroopers were more or less regarded as cattle and sheep stealers only. A general act for the better prosecution of thieves and highwaymen, in 1653, offered rewards of £10 per man, particularly for *"felons known as moss troopers residing on the Borders of England and Scotland."* Unfortunately this proved to have little effect and the problem dragged on until a commission was set up in 1672 which brought matters to a climax by 1676, when 33 Armstrongs and Elliots were exiled to Ireland. As one Armstrong poignantly wrote:

This is my departing night,
For here no longer must I stay;
There's neither friend nor foe of mine
But wishes me away.

What I have done through lack of wit,
I never, never can recall;
I hope you're all my good friends eyt;
Good night. And joy be with you all.

By 1681 things had calmed down considerably and today, as we enjoy the peace and tranquility of the Border country it is difficult to imagine its turbulent history, not only during the heyday of the Border reivers, but throughout its time as a frontier.

To capture the atmosphere of
THE BORDER REIVERS
why not visit some of the places listed overleaf.

There are many museums, former Border strongholds such as pele towers and castles, open to the public.

Or pick up a copy of the *Reivers Car Trail* from Carlisle visitor centre (see Page 56) and step back in time as you travel through Reiver Country and capture the sights and sounds of times gone by.

BORDER HISTORY MUSEUM

The Old Gaol, nr. Market Place, Hexham. Tel: 01434 604011

The Border History Museum is housed in the old gaol at Hexham. Built in 1330, from stones removed from Roman remains, this structure was the first purpose built gaol in England and remained in use as such until 1824.

At the first floor level, a combination of storyboards, photographs, models and weaponry is used to outline the life and times of the Border Reiver. Of particular interest is the original bastle house window donated by a friend of the museum. Other displays include the reputed skull of Sir John Fenwick. An audio commentary brings home the grim reality of 16th and 17th century border life.

The display on the second floor includes a replica of the interior of a border stronghold and the audio commentary describes the members of the Graham family of Liddlesdale in 1542.

OPEN: Easter - October: Mon. - Sat. 10.00a.m. to 4.30p.m.
(plus Sun., Spring Bank Holiday - Sept.)
February - Easter & November: Mon., Tues.,
10.00a.m. to 4.30p.m.
Party visits should be pre-booked.
No access for the disabled.

PRESTON TOWER

Chathill, Northumberland, NE67 5DH. Tel: 01665 589227
(7 miles north of Alnwick)

The tower was built by Sir Robert Harbottle in 1392 and is one of the few survivors of 78 pele towers listed in 1415. The tunnel vaulted rooms remain unaltered and provide a realistic picture of the grim way of life under the constant threat of the Border Reivers.
The accommodation provides a realistic picture of living conditions in a Border tower. The guardroom and prison are on the ground floor. On the first floor are a bedroom and living room both furnished as they might have been in the year 1400, and on the second floor is the Flodden room with a description of the battle, and extracts from Border history and ballads.

OPEN: All year - daylight hours.

CARLISLE VISITOR CENTRE

Old Town Hall, Greenmarket, Carlisle, CA3 8JH. Tel: 01228 512444

From here you can pick up a copy of the Reivers Car Trail (price: 50p). Use this leaflet to step back in time as you travel through approx. 80 miles of some of the most unspoilt and beautiful parts of Britain.

The route directions reflect the life of the late 20th century, but the descriptions of the surroundings are those of 1590. Imagine yourself back in time as you leave Carlisle and head for Bewcastle, Newcastleton, Hermitage Castle, the Debateable Lands...all in the heart of Border Reiver country.

OPEN: July & August: Mon. - Sat. 9.30a.m. to 7.00p.m.
Sun. 10.00a.m. to 5.00p.m.
May, June and Sept.: Mon. - Sat. 9.30a.m. to 6.30p.m.
Sun. 10.00a.m. to 5.00p.m.

TULLIE HOUSE CITY MUSEUM & ART GALLERY

Castle Street, Carlisle, CA3 8TP. Tel:01228 34781

Opened on 6th January 1991, Tullie House is one of Britain's most innovative historic attractions.

Portraying Carlisle's fascinating and turbulent place in Border history, the galleries captivate and enthrall visitors of all ages, with the power of their images, objects, stories and hands-on displays.

The museum focuses on the Romans, the historic railways and the notorious Border Reivers.

OPEN: all year except Christmas Day
From 10.00a.m. Monday to Saturday
From 12 noon on Sunday.
Facilities for the disabled.

CARLISLE CASTLE

Tel: 01228 31777

An exploration of the steep staircases and dark passageways of this proud border fortress, gives you an insight into the troubled years of the border wars.

English Heritage

Open: Apr. -Sept. 9.30.a.m. to 6.00p.m.

1st Oct. - 31st Mar. 9.30a.m. to 4.00p.m.

LIDDLESDALE HERITAGE CENTRE

South Hermitage St.,
Newcastleton.
Tel: 013873 75391

This attractive historical display portrays the history of Liddlesdale and its people.

Open: Easter - end Sept. daily (except Tues.)

CLAN ARMSTRONG TRUST CENTRE

Janet Armstrong House,
Douglas Sq., Newcastleton.
Tel: 013873 71593

The Centre houses the world's largest collection of Armstrong memorabilia from the 12th century through to the Border Reivers of Liddlesdale and the Western marches and beyond.

OPEN: Easter weekend, Whit - end Sept. 6 days a week 1.30. - 4.30p.m.
Closed : Monday.

HERMITAGE CASTLE

5.5m. NE of Newcastleton, off the A7, or by B6399

An awe-inspiring 14th century fortress at the centre of many of the bloodiest events in the turbulent history of the Borders. It was built by the de Soulis family before the end of the 13th century and history records a succession of Nevilles, Douglases and Dacres as Lords of Hermitage.

James IV passed the castle to the Earls of Bothwell and Francis 'King Devil' Bothwell, reputed to be a witch, used it as a 'safe' house for his plundering and reiving until it was taken back by the crown in 1594.

OPEN: Apr. - Sept. : Mon.-Sat. 9.30a.m. to 6.30p.m.
Sun: 2.00p.m. to 6.30p.m.
Oct. - Mar. : Saturday & Sunday only.

GILNOCKIE TOWER

Canonbie, DG14 0XD.

The Armstrong Clan maintain a clan room at Gilnockie (or Hollows Tower), traditionally claimed to be the home of Johnny Armstrong.

The room is decorated with the clan insignia and standard, and a painting of the tower commissioned by the new Laird. Around the walls are charts illustrating the descent of some of the clan, maps showing the Border area and the location of the Clans.

The tower is open by appointment - please give at least 7 days notice of your visit by writing to the tower at the above address.

SMAILHOLM TOWER

6m. west of Kelso, near Smailholm village. B6937.

A well-preserved and attractive 16th century tower house set on a high rocky knoll. It houses a permanent exhibition of tapestries and costume dolls depicting characters from Sir Walter Scott's 'Minstrelsy of the Scottish Borders'. The tower belonged to the Scott family and as a boy Sir Walter visited the adjacent farmhouse.

OPEN: Apr. - Sept. Mon. to Sat. 9.30a.m. - 6.30p.m.
Sun. 2.00p.m. - 6.30p.m. Closed in winter.

If you have enjoyed these tales of the Border Reivers, the following books published by Sandhill Press offer a more comprehensive history of the time.

Also published by Sandhill Press

ANGLO SAXON NORTHUMBRIA
by T.H. Rowland
Explore the Golden Age of Northumbria through this vivid account of a significant period in our history: the dawning of Christianity, the Contest of Kings, the terrible destruction of the Viking raids.
Paperback ISBN 0 946098 34 4 £2.99

THE BIGGEST MINING VILLAGE IN THE WORLD
by Mike Kirkup
This social history, largely based on the reminiscences of north east pitmen and their families, provides a unique opportunity to examine the origins of the coal industry and one particular coal town: Ashington.
Paperback ISBN 0 946098 30 1 £9.95

THE BODY IN THE BANK: Famous Northern Murders
Retold by Sandhill Press
A fascinating collection of murders, trials and subsequent harsh punishments which took place in our northern towns and countryside.
Paperback ISBN 0 946098 33 6 £1.95

CUSTOMS AND TRADITIONS OF NORTHUMBRIA
Retold by Sandhill Press
Customs & traditions associated with ceremonies, seasons and times of the year, leisure and work activities are all investigated, and popular superstitions are recounted.
Paperback ISBN 0 946098 28 X £1.95

THE GREAT GUNMAKER : the life of Lord Armstrong
by David Dougan
A fascinating biography of William Armstrong, one of the nineteenth century's leading arms manufacturers.
Paperback ISBN 0 946098 23 9 £5.95

Also published by Sandhill Press

IN AND AROUND
ALNWICK...MORPETH...ROTHBURY...WARKWORTH
by Ian Smith
First in a new series in which Ian explores Northumberland's towns, villages and their rivers. Written in Ian's inimatable style, the book also includes his own line drawings and maps.
(Warkworth section also published separately)
Paperback ISBN 0 946098 26 3 £3.95

MYTH AND MAGIC OF NORTHUMBRIA
Retold by Sandhill Press
Wizards and witches, fairies and sprites, charms and spells - a retelling of strange happenings from Northumbria's folklore.
Paperback ISBN 0 946098 27 1 £1.95

NORTHUMBERLAND PLACE NAMES
by Godfrey Watson
Through the names of towns and villages, farms and shepherds' huts, the fascinating history of Northumberland is revealed.
Paperback ISBN 0 946098 38 7 £6.95

NORTHUMBRIA IN PICTURES
by Beryl Sanderson
A new revised edition of our successful colour souvenir guide - 40 superb colour photographs and accompanying text.
Hardback ISBN 0 946098 22 0 £11.95

NORTHUMBRIAN COASTLINE
by Ian Smith
Now in its 2nd revised edition, Ian's hugely successful guide - over 14,000 copies sold - covers the area from Berwick upon Tweed to North Shields.
Paperback ISBN 0 946098 32 8 £3.95

Also published by Sandhill Press

NORTHUMBRIAN NATURE DIARY
by Wendy Dickson Illus. by John Steele
From January to December, this delightful diary records some of Northumberland's wonderful wildlife.
Paperback ISBN 0 946098 31 X £3.99

THE NORTHUMBRIAN PUB : an architectural history
by Lynn F. Pearson
An examination of why Northumbrian pubs look as they do today.
Hardback ISBN 0 946098 15 8 £4.95 (Reduced from £15.95)

UPPER COQUETDALE
by David Dippie Dixon
Northumberland : its history, traditions, folklore and scenery.
Originally published in 1903 - a special limited numbered edition.
Hardback ISBN 0 946098 07 7 £19.95

VICTORIAN AND EDWARDIAN NORTHUMBRIA FROM OLD PHOTOGRAPHS
by J.W. Thompson and D. Bond
Hardback ISBN 0 946098 08 5 £7.95

WARKWORTH
by Ian Smith
A charming guide to this unique Northumbrian village.
Paperback ISBN 0 946098 21 2 £1.50

WATERS OF TYNE
by T.H. Rowland
Following the various sources of the Tyne to the North Sea, the book charts the changes to and by the river throughout history.
Paperback ISBN 0 946098 36 0 £6.99